Original title:
After the End

Copyright © 2024 Swan Charm
All rights reserved.

Author: Kene Elistrand
ISBN HARDBACK: 978-9916-89-933-5
ISBN PAPERBACK: 978-9916-89-934-2
ISBN EBOOK: 978-9916-89-935-9

Tales of the Healing Wind

In the whisper of the breeze, we find,
Gentle blessings on our weary minds.
Healing comes through faith and grace,
In every touch, the divine embrace.

Winds carry prayers across the sea,
A sacred hymn, a call to be free.
The heart awakens, the soul takes flight,
In every sigh, the promise of light.

Nature's breath brings solace anew,
From the mountains high to the waters blue.
In the rustling leaves, a chorus sings,
Echoes of joy in the song of spring.

With each gust, our burdens are shed,
In the dance of life, we are gently led.
To the healing wind, we raise our hands,
United as one, in faith we stand.

So let us walk where the shadows fade,
In the light of love, our fears persuade.
Through the whispers of the sky so wide,
We find our hope, our hearts as guide.

Testament of the Followed Star

A star shines bright in the weary night,
Guiding souls through the darkest fight.
With a glow of promise, it lights the way,
For those who long for a brand new day.

Each twinkle tells of dreams pursued,
Of faith enduring, of love imbued.
In silence, we heed its quiet call,
A beacon of hope illuminating all.

The journey begins beneath its gaze,
With courage kindled in faith's blaze.
Walking onward, we trust the path,
In the light of the star, escape the wrath.

Through trials faced and sorrows shared,
The followed star shows we are cared.
In every heart, a quiet flame,
A testament to the sacred name.

So let us follow where it leads us still,
In the night so vast, we find our will.
With every step, our spirits soared,
In the glow of love, forever adored.

The Altar of Unseen Sacrifice

On bended knee, we humbly pray,
In the silence, our fears decay.
An altar built with love and tears,
Holding our hopes through the passing years.

Each sacrifice, a whisper made,
In shadows cast, our hearts displayed.
We give our all in unseen grace,
Trusting in truth, we find our place.

In the night, the spirits rise,
Offering strength beyond the skies.
For every loss, a blessing found,
In the depths of faith, our hearts are bound.

With open hands, we dare to trust,
In the sacred bond, we place our gust.
For in every hardship, we find the light,
Through unseen sacrifice, we ignite.

So gather close, let love abide,
In the altar's warmth, we shall confide.
With every heartbeat, our vows renew,
In the sacred stillness, love's journey is true.

Chronicles of Eternal Return

In the circle of time, we gather near,
Chronicles written, stories clear.
We journey forth, then back again,
In the sacred cycle, we understand.

Life unfolds like a fragrant bloom,
In every season, we embrace the room.
With echoes of laughter, shadows of pain,
In the heart of existence, all we gain.

Through the sands of time, our spirits weave,
A tapestry rich, we learn to believe.
In the folds of the past, the future shines,
In every heartbeat, divinity aligns.

So let us dance through dusk and dawn,
With every step, our fears are gone.
For in the rhythm of life we find,
Eternal return, forever entwined.

In the quiet moments, truth reveals,
The stories of hope that destiny seals.
Together we rise, in love we learn,
In the chronicles of life, we eternally yearn.

Echoes of an Eternal Dawn

In the stillness, whispers rise,
Promises of light fill the skies.
Hearts awaken with fervent plea,
Bathed in grace, forever free.

Morning breaks with gentle hand,
Guiding souls to sacred land.
In the warmth, shadows fall,
Love and mercy cover all.

Each step taken, faith ignites,
Through the darkness, purest sights.
Guided by a glowing spark,
Life reborn within the ark.

With every breath, a hymn we sing,
Offering to the One, our King.
In His presence, hope resounds,
Echoes of an eternal dawn.

Rebirth in the Ashen Light

From ashes, life begins to bloom,
A fragrant hope dispels the gloom.
In the depths of trials faced,
New horizons are embraced.

With faith's fire, we shall rise,
Beneath the vast and open skies.
Transcending all that came before,
Hearts united, spirits soar.

In shadows deep, the light will gleam,
A promise whispered in the dream.
Rebirth springs from pain endured,
In His love, we are assured.

Each moment, a chance to renew,
Through the storm, we walk in His view.
With every step, we find our way,
In the ash, we live to pray.

The Sanctuary of Lost Souls

In valleys deep where silence reigns,
The weary seek to share their pains.
A sanctuary, built with care,
Embracing all who wander there.

With gentle hands, they are restored,
In mercy's grace, they find their reward.
Every heart, a story shared,
In the refuge, love is declared.

Through trials faced and burdens borne,
A light emerges, hope reborn.
In sacred space, the past will fade,
As faith in unity is laid.

Lost souls gather, hand in hand,
Together forged, a faithful band.
In this haven, joy unfolds,
A testament of love retold.

Celestial Voices in the Void

In the silence, echoes call,
Celestial whispers touch us all.
Beyond the stars, the truth prevails,
Guiding hearts on faith's soft trails.

Each voice a beacon, shining bright,
In the vast expanse of night.
Drawing near with every breath,
Life's sweet promise conquers death.

Through the void, we seek the light,
Awakening souls with pure delight.
In the stillness, courage grows,
From endless depths, our spirit flows.

In harmony, we rise and sing,
Of love eternal, our offering.
Together bound, through the divine,
Celestial voices intertwine.

Beyond the Dust of Forgetting

In shadows deep where silence dwells,
The echoes of our spirit tells.
Through trials faced and sorrows known,
A light emerges, hope has grown.

Each tear we shed, a seed of grace,
Transcending time, no soul laid waste.
In whispered prayers, our faith ignites,
A guiding star in endless nights.

What once was lost, will yet be found,
In sacred space, our hearts unbound.
Beyond the veil of pain and fear,
Eternal love, forever near.

So rise, O spirit, break the chain,
Embrace the joy amidst the pain.
Through dust of years, our truths unite,
In holy bonds, we find the light.

The Prayer of Wandering Hearts

In search of peace, our journey starts,
With open hands and wandering hearts.
Through valleys low and mountains high,
We seek the grace that fills the sky.

Each step we take, a prayer we make,
In whispers soft, our souls awake.
For every doubt, a faith reborn,
In love's embrace, we'll not feel worn.

Through trials faced and lessons learned,
The flame of hope within us burned.
A bond unbroken, strong and true,
In unity, we rise anew.

So guide us, Lord, through shadows cast,
With every heartbeat, hold us fast.
For wandering hearts, your light imparts,
The dream of home where love restarts.

Realms of Reawakening

In realms where dreams and visions dwell,
A sacred truth begins to swell.
With every breath, life's vast design,
Awakens spirits, pure and divine.

The dawn breaks forth, a whisper sweet,
As hearts once cold begin to beat.
In nature's grace, we find our call,
To rise in love, to never fall.

Embrace the light of every star,
For distance fades, and near we are.
The essence flows like rivers wide,
In unity, we'll turn the tide.

No fear can bind the soul that's free,
In love's embrace, we'll always be.
Awake, arise, for hope is near,
In realms of grace, we shed our fear.

A Chorus for the Unsung

In every heart, a story lies,
A voice unheard beneath the skies.
For those who toil in shadows deep,
A chorus stirs, their truths to keep.

With every silent tear they shed,
A symphony of hope is bred.
Through struggle's grip, they find their song,
In unity, where they belong.

Their dreams take flight on wings of grace,
A tapestry of every face.
Though unsung, their spirits soar,
In love's embrace, they are restored.

O let the world now hear their cry,
For every heart can learn to fly.
A chorus strong, it daily sings,
To lift our souls on joyous wings.

Mosaic of the Universe Reborn

In the canvas of the night,
Stars weave tales of ancient light.
Every spark, a soul set free,
In the dance of eternity.

Colors blend in holy sphere,
Whispers of the heart, so clear.
Each fragment, a sacred call,
Unity in love's sweet thrall.

From ashes rise in sacred breath,
Bringing life to shadows of death.
The cosmos spins, in His embrace,
Finding beauty in His grace.

Across the void of space and time,
Creation sings in rhythm and rhyme.
Every moment, a piece reborn,
In the dawn of solace, light is sworn.

In reverence, we stand and gaze,
At the wonder of His ways.
This mosaic bright and alive,
Together in faith, we will thrive.

The Tides of a New Heaven

Beneath the waves where silence thrives,
Heaven whispers in our lives.
Every ebb, a prayer sent,
In love's embrace, we are content.

The moon guides the sea's deep song,
In its rhythm, we belong.
Each tide, a promise, strong and true,
Reflecting grace in every hue.

As we sail on faith's vast sea,
In storms, we find serenity.
With hope your anchor, trust your sail,
In the journey's heart, we shall prevail.

The shores of light await our tread,
With every step, the path is led.
New heaven calls, as we ascend,
In its embrace, there's no end.

In this voyage, souls unite,
Guided by the stars so bright.
Together in love's everlasting tide,
In Him, forever we shall abide.

Pilgrimage to the Unfathomable

Upon the path, our feet are led,
Where sacred whispers long have tread.
Every step, a heartbeat grows,
Into the heart where mercy flows.

Mountains high and valleys low,
Toward the truth, our spirits glow.
Each mile, a lesson learned in grace,
In this pilgrimage, we find our place.

With open hearts, we journey on,
Through twilight's veil, before the dawn.
Beneath the weight of faith we walk,
In silent prayer, our spirits talk.

The unfathomable waits ahead,
In love's embrace, no fear, no dread.
With each encounter, wisdom shines,
In the light of sacred signs.

Together, we rise, hand in hand,
Bound by the sacred, a holy band.
In this quest, our souls ignite,
Finding the divine in every light.

Harmonies of the Resurrected

In the garden, blooms anew,
Life arises, fresh with dew.
Every flower, a promise made,
In the dawn, our fears allayed.

Voices sing in joyful refrain,
Echoes of love, free from pain.
Each note, a testament to grace,
Resurrection's warm embrace.

Hearts entwined in sacred song,
Together where we all belong.
In every struggle, we shall rise,
Li¬ght of hope fills darkened skies.

From shadows past, we walk in light,
In the stillness, find our sight.
With faith as our compass, we advance,
In the rhythms of a holy dance.

In every spirit, hope ignites,
Through the silence, faith ignites.
Harmonies of life shall weave,
In love eternal, we believe.

The Spirit's Ascent

In quiet chambers, whispers rise,
Heavenly light, breaks through the skies.
Hearts ignited, by love's embrace,
Souls united, in sacred space.

Wings unfurled, on faith's own breath,
Carried forth, beyond the death.
To realms where mercy flows like streams,
In hope's soft glow, we weave our dreams.

Mountains tremble, as we behold,
The sacred stories, of ages old.
In every heartbeat, the echoes sing,
Of wondrous grace, the angels bring.

Through trials faced, and sorrows steep,
In every prayer, our spirits leap.
With every step, towards the divine,
In unity, our souls align.

Ascend we shall, on wings anew,
Into the light, forever true.
In love's pure flame, our spirits soar,
To heights unknown, forevermore.

Exodus into Eternity

Crossing the sands, with faith as guide,
In every heart, the spirit resides.
We walk in courage, hand in hand,
Towards the promise, of the land.

Stars above, in glory shine,
Leading our steps, divine design.
With every heartbeat, echoes of grace,
In the journey's midst, we find our place.

Chains of darkness, cast away,
In the light of hope, we find our sway.
With trust in the unseen, we rise,
Towards the horizon, the soul complies.

Through valleys deep, and mountains high,
With faith we wander, hearts on fire.
Each trial faced, a lesson learned,
In every tear, the heart has yearned.

Together we march, into the dawn,
In unity's strength, we carry on.
With every step, toward eternity,
In love's embrace, we are set free.

Veils of Grace and Grit

In shadows cast, where faith does dwell,
The whispers of grace, we know so well.
Through trials tough, we stand as one,
In every struggle, God's will be done.

Veils of doubt, we cast aside,
In strength and hope, our hearts abide.
Each breath a prayer, each tear a seed,
In unity's bond, we find our creed.

Bridges built, with love and trust,
We rise from ashes, as hope is a must.
In every challenge, we find our voice,
In life's grand tapestry, we rejoice.

With grit we climb, the steepest hills,
In heaven's light, our spirit fills.
Through thick and thin, we wander bold,
In hopes reborn, our stories told.

Embracing grace, amidst the fight,
With hearts aglow, we seek the light.
Through veils we see, the truth within,
In faith's embrace, our lives begin.

The Resurrection of Dreams

In silent night, where wishes dwell,
A gentle whisper, a sacred spell.
From ashes rise, the dreams once lost,
In love's embrace, we bear the cost.

Hope ignites, like morning dew,
With every dawn, we start anew.
In deeper faith, our spirits gleam,
Awakening now, the sacred dream.

Through darkest times, our souls endure,
In every trial, we find the cure.
With every heartbeat, a promise made,
In shadows cast, our fears must fade.

Weaving futures, with threads of grace,
In every tear, God's touch we trace.
Through valleys low, to mountains high,
In every struggle, we learn to fly.

The resurrection, of dreams anew,
In love's embrace, we find our view.
With faith as guide, our hearts take flight,
Into the dawn, we chase the light.

The Last Breath of the Forgotten

In silence lies the voice of prayer,
Forgotten souls who tread the flare.
Their whispers rise to heaven's gate,
A plea for mercy, a chance, a fate.

In shadows deep, where hope does wane,
Faith flickers soft, through joy and pain.
Each breath released, a story told,
Of love that lingers, and hearts so bold.

In twilight's grasp, the stars align,
To guide the lost, through realms divine.
Their paths unknown, yet spirits soar,
To find the grace they've longed for more.

As echoes fade, the world does pause,
Awakening hearts to ancient cause.
In every sorrow, in every strife,
The last breath holds the spark of life.

Celestial Gardens in Ruins

Where once the blooms in splendor grew,
Now barren ground, and skies of blue.
The petals fall like sacred tears,
Bearing witness to lost years.

The angels sigh beneath the trees,
In whispered hymns upon the breeze.
Each root may twist in tangled night,
Yet holds a promise of future light.

From ashes rise the seeds of grace,
In broken earth, the holy space.
For every loss, a chance to heal,
An inner bloom, our hearts reveal.

Though shadows creep and darkness looms,
The spirit casts away the glooms.
In gardens torn, hope's bright refrain,
Awaits the storm, embraces rain.

So let us tend the fields of dreams,
With faith that flows in golden streams.
In ruins still, the light will gleam,
Celestial visions, a wish, a dream.

Hymns of the Second Coming

Awake the hearts, let voices raise,
In sacred tune, recall the praise.
For in the dawn of holy days,
We sing of hope, eternal ways.

The clouds assemble, the angels near,
With every note, dispel the fear.
In joyous throngs, we stand together,
Embracing love that lasts forever.

The bells may toll, the world may weep,
Yet through it all, our faith we keep.
With open arms, we greet the light,
As shadows fade and dreams take flight.

From every corner, voices ring,
A symphony of peace we bring.
In melodies, our spirits soar,
A hymn resounding, forevermore.

So let us gather, hand in hand,
To witness grace throughout the land.
For in each song, the truth shall gleam,
The promise held in every dream.

Beneath the Shattered Halo

Beneath the crown of golden light,
Lie souls in search of sacred sight.
With fallen words and broken wings,
They weave through tales that silence brings.

In every tear, a story flows,
Of battles fought, and love that grows.
The halo cracked, yet still it shines,
A testament to tangled lines.

In shadows cast, we seek to feel,
The warmth of grace, the chance to heal.
For even broken, we are whole,
A spirit's light within the soul.

And while the world may turn to dust,
In shattered forms, we find our trust.
For love transcends the deepest night,
Beneath the halo, we embrace the light.

So gather near, and lift your gaze,
To skies adorned with hope ablaze.
In every heart, a flicker glows,
A promise kept as love bestows.

Echoes of Divine Solitude

In silence, whispers of grace rise,
Hearts awaken under starlit skies.
The stillness, a sacred embrace,
Guides the soul to a holy space.

Within the shadows, light takes flight,
In corridors of truth, pure and bright.
Each breath a prayer, a gentle sign,
Of love that flows through the divine.

The echoes of ages softly call,
In the heart's quiet, we find it all.
Every tear a step toward peace,
In solitude, our souls release.

In every storm, a tranquil eye,
A promise woven in the sky.
Faith, a river flowing deep,
In divine solitude, our spirits leap.

Together we walk, hand in hand,
On this hallowed, sacred land.
Embracing whispers, ever near,
In echoes of solitude, we hear.

Rebirth Amongst the Ruins

From ashes, hope begins to bloom,
Where shadows linger, light finds room.
In broken stones, life seeks to rise,
A testament to love that never dies.

Each fracture speaks of battles fought,
In every scar, a lesson taught.
With faith like roots that delve so deep,
Amongst the ruins, our hearts shall leap.

The sunrise spills across the gray,
A symphony of light's display.
In rubble's cradle, dreams ignite,
A rebirth born from darkest night.

With each soft step upon the earth,
We hold the promise of rebirth.
In whispered prayers, we find our way,
Amongst the ruins, hope's bright ray.

Together we rise, not alone,
In every heart, the truth is sown.
With open arms, we greet the dawn,
Rebirth, a song forever drawn.

Sanctuaries of the Forgotten

In whispers of leaves, the stories lie,
Of sacred places, where spirits fly.
Amongst the moss, old memories creep,
In sanctuaries forgotten, we keep.

The stones, they carry a gentle weight,
Of prayers once spoken, sealing fate.
In broken walls, the echoes sing,
Of faith enduring, eternal spring.

Beneath the arches, shadows sway,
Where once the light would dance and play.
In quietude, the heart confides,
In forgotten sanctuaries, love abides.

Each wanderer will find a trail,
A path through journeys made of frail.
In reverent silence, we shall seek,
The solace found in the meek and weak.

So let us kneel in humble grace,
In every corner, a holy space.
With every heartbeat, a gentle nod,
To sanctuaries of the forgotten, we trod.

Pilgrimage to the Subtle Light

Through valleys deep, where shadows play,
 We wander forth, both night and day.
  With every step, a soul's desire,
  A pilgrimage to the light we aspire.

 The road is long, yet fiercely bright,
With faith as our guide, we seek the right.
  In murmurs soft, the heavens call,
   To the subtle light, we give our all.

 In every moment, the heart discovers,
   In unity, we become like brothers.
  With hopes entwined, we tread as one,
   Towards horizons kissed by the sun.

   The journey tells of trials faced,
    In every tear, a victory graced.
Yet through the struggle, we find our might,
  A pilgrimage unfolds to the subtle light.

    So let us gather, hand in hand,
     In sacred trust, we understand.
    With open eyes, we seek to find,
 The subtle light, embracing all mankind.

The Horizon of New Hopes

In dawn's embrace the light appears,
A canvas bright of change and cheer.
The shadows flee, the heart takes wing,
With faith anew, the soul shall sing.

Each step we take on this fresh ground,
In unity of hope we're bound.
The trials faced, the lessons learned,
In every heart, a fire burned.

The winds of grace, they call our name,
In whispered tones, we rise the same.
With open arms, we seek the skies,
A journey true, where love complies.

From humble roots, our spirits soar,
In kindness shared, we seek for more.
Together we shall light the way,
With every step, we greet the day.

In faith we sow, our dreams abound,
A tapestry of hope is found.
The horizon glows, a path so bright,
As we embrace the endless light.

Whispers from the Infinite

In silence deep, the echoes flow,
A melody, through night and glow.
The stars align, the sacred sound,
In whispers soft, the truth is found.

The universe, a sacred breath,
In every pulse, in life and death.
A dance of light, a cosmic grace,
In every heart, we find our place.

With open mind, we seek and yearn,
The wisdom shared, the lessons learned.
In every word, a bridge is made,
To touch the souls, their fears allayed.

The infinite speaks, in every dawn,
A promise held, a light reborn.
With courage bold, we shall not fear,
For love will guide us, ever near.

The gentle breeze, it calls our name,
In whispered tones, we rise the same.
Through storms that rage, and trials long,
In faith we find, our hearts are strong.

The Wellspring of Renewed Faith

In valleys low, where shadows creep,
The well of hope, awakens deep.
A springing forth of life and grace,
In every heart, a sacred space.

The water flows, a gentle stream,
Refreshing souls, igniting dreams.
With every drop, a story told,
Of love and faith, in days of old.

From barren lands, new blossoms rise,
In every color, we find the skies.
With roots embedded, we stand tall,
Together bound, we rise and call.

The light spills forth, a golden hue,
In every moment, born anew.
A symphony of heart and mind,
In love we trust, our souls aligned.

With every ripple, peace is found,
In unity, all hearts are sound.
The wellspring flows, forever bright,
A beacon true, in darkest night.

Whispers of the Twilight Realm

In twilight's hush, the spirits sigh,
They share the dreams that never die.
A soft embrace, the shadows weave,
In every heart, their truths believe.

As lanterns glow with sacred light,
The stars align on this holy night.
A gentle breeze, a whispered prayer,
Invites the faithful to repair.

In every moment, grace sustains,
Through trials faced, love breaks the chains.
The spirit's song, a guiding call,
In twilight's realm, we rise, not fall.

The veil is thin, we sense the grace,
In every soul, a sacred space.
With open hearts, we seek and find,
The whispers soft, forever kind.

So let your faith like rivers flow,
Through valleys deep and mountains low.
In twilight's realm, here we abide,
With every breath, our souls collide.

Cherubic Echoes of Tomorrow

The dawn reveals a promise bright,
Cherubic echoes take their flight.
With laughter pure and joyful grace,
They lead the way to sacred space.

In gentle tones, a hymn shall rise,
A melody that never dies.
In every heart, their whispers dwell,
A sacred truth we yearn to tell.

With wings of hope, they soar above,
A testament of faith and love.
In each embrace, the light ignites,
A beacon shining through the nights.

As blossoms bloom in sacred spring,
Their light shines forth, our spirits sing.
With every step, we walk in grace,
Cherubic echoes, our warm embrace.

Tomorrow's promise gently calls,
With open arms, the spirit falls.
To grasp the truth in every sigh,
We rise, we grow, we never die.

Redemption's Dawn

As morning breaks, redemption's near,
The shadows fade, the skies are clear.
With every heartbeat, grace unfolds,
A tale of mercy, brave and bold.

Forgiveness flows like rivers wide,
In love's embrace, we all abide.
With every tear, a healing balm,
In quiet strength, we find our calm.

The sun ascends, our spirits rise,
A chorus sweet, our voices prize.
In faith united, we shall stand,
With hearts aligned, we walk the land.

The past is veiled, a distant shore,
In every soul, redemption's door.
We break the chains and lift our eyes,
To greet the dawn and claim our prize.

In every heartbeat, hope is born,
The world anew, redemption's dawn.
With hands held high, our spirits soar,
In love, we find forevermore.

Ascension Beyond the Veil

With every sigh, the spirit takes,
A journey grand, where silence breaks.
Beyond the veil, the souls unite,
In radiant arms, they find the light.

In cosmic dance, we twirl and glide,
Through endless love, we shall abide.
In every heartbeat, grace bestows,
The sacred truth the heart now knows.

From earthly chains, we are set free,
Emerging bright, our spirits see.
As whispers softly guide our way,
In unity, we find our stay.

Where time dissolves, our souls expand,
In boundless love, forever stand.
In every glance, divinity gleams,
Beyond the veil, we weave our dreams.

So let our hearts ascend and soar,
In realms of light, forevermore.
With every breath, we rise as one,
Ascension calls, our time has come.

Wings of Hope in Desolation

In valleys deep where sorrow reigns,
Angels whisper soft refrains.
Their wings lift hearts from pain's embrace,
Revealing light, divine grace.

When shadows loom and courage wanes,
Faith like a river breaks the chains.
Through darkest nights the spirit soars,
Finding peace beyond closed doors.

With every tear, a prayer ascends,
A promise that the heart transcends.
In desolation, hope ignites,
Guiding souls to sacred heights.

For in the silence, love prevails,
A beacon bright when courage fails.
Hold fast to dreams, let not them fade,
For wings of hope cannot be swayed.

The Garden of Everlasting Light

In gardens where the lilies bloom,
Resilience thrums, dispelling gloom.
Each petal sings of grace bestowed,
In every heart, love's seed is sowed.

The sunbeams dance on golden rays,
Guiding souls through endless days.
With every step on sacred ground,
In silence, God's presence is found.

Amidst the thorns, sweet roses grow,
As faith reveals the beauty's glow.
A tapestry of light and care,
Enfolds, unites, in joyful prayer.

In sacred spaces, souls connect,
A tranquil hush where hearts reflect.
For in His garden, love ignites,
Eternal peace in heavenly sights.

The Pilgrim's Return to Grace

A pilgrim walks through dust and stone,
With weary feet, but never alone.
Each step unveils a path of light,
Guided by faith through darkest night.

The echoes of the past may call,
Yet hope stands firm, lest we should fall.
A journey marked with trials faced,
Leads weary hearts back to grace embraced.

With every trial, wisdom's gain,
In valleys low, we find refrain.
For every tear, a lesson learned,
In pilgrim's soul, true faith is earned.

The road ahead may twist and turn,
Yet flames of joy within us burn.
Return to grace, O wandering heart,
In love's warm grasp, you'll never part.

Shadows Transformed by Faith

In shadows cast where doubts arise,
Faith's gentle light unveils the skies.
Each whispered prayer, a thread of gold,
Transforms the darkness; love unfolds.

With every trial, strength is built,
In broken moments, grace is spilt.
Through shadows deep, our spirits rise,
The dawn of hope, where love complies.

In the silence, we find our voice,
In faith's embrace, we make our choice.
To travel forth with hearts made new,
In shadows' dance, we seek the true.

For every burden shared in prayer,
Transforms our burdens, lightens care.
Through shadows cast, we walk in light,
Faith guides us true, eternal right.

The Light Within the Abyss

In shadows deep where fears reside,
A flicker glows, a hope to guide.
Though darkness reigns, the heart's embrace,
Shall illuminate, grant strength and grace.

Amid the chaos, whispers call,
A sacred light defies the fall.
From depths of sorrow, faith ignites,
To turn the night to vibrant sights.

Within the void, a spark appears,
Transforming doubts to endless cheers.
Each step through trials, we align,
With light that dances, pure divine.

The abyss may seem a daunting fate,
Yet, still we rise to radiate.
For within us dwells that blazing flame,
To conquer dark and break the chain.

So when despair attempts to claim,
Remember well, we're not the same.
The light within shall never cease,
To guide us all, to grant us peace.

Parables from the Ashes

From dust we rise, in quiet grace,
Each story told, an embrace.
Lives entwined through trials faced,
In ashes found, our hope replaced.

The fire burns, a lesson learned,
In bitter strife, our spirits turned.
Through suffering, the soul shall grow,
To touch the skies, to seek the glow.

Wisdom whispers in the night,
In darkest times, we find the light.
The past may haunt, but skies will clear,
Parables dawn, hope drawing near.

Each scar a tale of battles fought,
In every heart, a truth is sought.
For from the ashes, seeds will bloom,
Transforming loss to life's perfume.

So let the winds of change arise,
With open hearts and lifted eyes.
We walk the path with faith restored,
In every step, the soul adored.

Reverent Shadows of a New Dawn

In stillness found, the morning breaks,
As shadows fade, the heart awakes.
With reverence, we greet the sun,
A brand new day has just begun.

The whispers of the night depart,
While light ignites the sleeping heart.
Each dawn a gift, a chance to grow,
In sacred ways, the spirit flows.

With gentle hands, the earth is kissed,
By light divine, we can't resist.
In every shadow, grace shall dwell,
To guide our living, cast a spell.

As warmth envelops all in sight,
We seek to walk in truth and light.
With reverent hearts, we stand in awe,
Of all that's pure and filled with law.

So let us dance in morning's glow,
Embrace the joys, let kindness grow.
In shadows past, we find our way,
Towards a brighter, blessed day.

Sanctity in Silent Desolation

In quiet gloom, where echoes lie,
A sacred truth begins to sigh.
Within the void, we seek a song,
Of sacred peace where souls belong.

Desolation holds a distant grace,
In whispered winds, we find our place.
Through stillness, hearts begin to see,
The sanctity of being free.

Though silence grips, and shadows loom,
In every corner, love will bloom.
For in the dark, a light does gleam,
Reviving hope, a tender dream.

We gather strength from broken pasts,
In gentle breaths, our quiet casts.
With open arms, let souls be known,
In desolation, seeds are sown.

So let us walk with grace anew,
In solemn paths where light breaks through.
For even here, life's beauty sings,
In sanctity, our spirit springs.

Threads Woven in Sacred Silence

In quietude, our spirits meet,
A tapestry where hearts retreat.
Each whispered prayer, a sacred thread,
In the loom of faith, we are gently led.

Beneath the stars, the shadows dance,
In holy stillness, we find our chance.
To weave our hopes in night's embrace,
A woven symphony, divine grace.

With each soft breath, the silence grows,
In sacred spaces, love bestows.
Threads of mercy intertwine,
In the heart's fabric, the light will shine.

The sacred whispers, secrets shared,
In the silence, our souls are bared.
Threads of joy and threads of pain,
In the quietude, we find the gain.

And so we gather, hearts entwined,
In the sacred silence, truth defined.
A canvas painted with faith's design,
In this holy moment, love will align.

Beneath the Gaze of the Unseen

Beneath the gaze of the unseen light,
Our spirits wander through the night.
In shadows deep, we seek the grace,
Guided by faith in this sacred space.

The whispers of hope, like gentle wind,
In the silence, our journey begins.
With humble hearts, we yearn to see,
The truth that lies in eternity.

In every moment, a chance to rise,
As love unfolds, we realize.
The unseen presence, ever near,
In faith's embrace, we cast our fear.

Each step we take, a prayer in motion,
A river flowing, deep as ocean.
With eyes unclouded, we seek the dawn,
Beneath the gaze, our fears are gone.

And as the stars begin to gleam,
In quiet awe, we dare to dream.
Beneath this gaze, we find our way,
In the light of love, we choose to stay.

The Daybreak of the Soul

As morning breaks with soft embrace,
The day begins its gentle race.
With every sunbeam, hope takes flight,
Awakening the soul with light.

In whispered prayers, the dawn arrives,
A canvas bright where spirit thrives.
Each golden ray, a sacred call,
In the light of love, we stand tall.

With hearts aligned, we greet the morn,
In this new day, the spirit is born.
Each moment glimmers, a chance to be,
In the daybreak's glow, we are set free.

In nature's song, the world awakes,
The beauty found in gentle breaks.
As shadows fade, we find our role,
In the sacred dawn, we find our soul.

Thus, we journey, hand in hand,
In the warmth of love, we take our stand.
The daybreak of the soul shall rise,
In the light of grace, see hope's disguise.

God's Canvas After Twilight

In twilight's hush, the colors blend,
A painter's grace, our hearts commend.
Each stroke a promise, soft and true,
On God's canvas, the world renews.

With shadows drawn, the stars ignite,
In the silence, we find the light.
The brush of faith sweeps wide and far,
As we gather near, beneath each star.

In the quiet dusk, our dreams take flight,
Reflections dance in the velvet night.
Each heartbeat echoes, a sacred sound,
On God's canvas, love abounds.

As night unfolds, the beauty grows,
A testament of all we chose.
With every breath, we paint the skies,
In the twilight's glow, our spirits rise.

And when the dawn begins to break,
In awe, we witness the love we make.
God's canvas, ever bright and wide,
In the twilight's grace, we abide.

The Ascent Beyond the Veil

With open hearts we seek the light,
To climb the path, divine and bright.
Beyond the veil where shadows fade,
In sacred grace, our souls remade.

Each step we take, a whispered prayer,
A promise kept to seek and care.
In unity, we rise and soar,
Over the hills, to heaven's door.

The truths revealed, in silence found,
In hallowed grounds where love is crowned.
With every breath, the spirit sings,
Embracing all the joy it brings.

A journey forged on faith's ascent,
Through trials faced, our hope is lent.
We climb with trust, our hearts alight,
United souls in endless flight.

Through realms unknown, with hearts ablaze,
In search of peace, we seek His gaze.
Upon the peaks, where angels dwell,
We find our truth, beyond the veil.

Celestial Journeys Unbound

In realms of dreams, our spirits glide,
Through cosmic seas, with love our guide.
Each star a spark of grace profound,
In celestial journeys, unbound.

The whispers of the heavens call,
As nights unfold, we heed the thrall.
In every glow, a tale to weave,
Of faith and hope, we dare believe.

The universe, a wondrous scroll,
Each planet hints of our true goal.
Through stardust paths, our hearts embrace,
The infinite, a sacred space.

With wings of prayer, we rise above,
In unity, we find our love.
The cosmic dance, a holy sign,
In every heartbeat, His design.

Through ancient trails where shadows roam,
We seek the light, a guiding home.
In sacred realms where spirits flow,
Celestial journeys help us grow.

Remnants of Light in the Gloom

Amidst the dark, a flicker glows,
A gentle warmth that softly flows.
Remnants of light, a beacon bright,
In shadow's grasp, still shines the right.

Through trials faced, our courage blooms,
In every heart, the spirit looms.
With steadfast faith, we pierce the night,
Finding the way to hope and light.

When sorrows weigh and doubts arise,
Look to the stars in asking skies.
For in the gloom, the heart shall find,
A whisper soft, love intertwined.

Each tear we shed, a sacred trace,
Of battles fought in grace's place.
In darkest hours, we shall ignite,
The remnants bright, to guide our sight.

So hand in hand, we journey true,
Emboldened by the light in you.
With every step, together loom,
The remnants shining in the gloom.

Labyrinths of Faith and Freedom

In winding paths of faith we roam,
Through labyrinths, we seek a home.
A quest for truth, our hearts desire,
In every turn, the sacred fire.

With open minds, we wander free,
In whispered winds, divinity.
Each choice we make, a dance of grace,
In unknown realms, we find our place.

The walls may close, yet hope will spark,
A guiding light within the dark.
Through faith's embrace, we break the chains,
In unity, the spirit gains.

With courage bold, we face each maze,
In love's embrace, our hearts we raise.
No fear can bind the soul that yearns,
For in this quest, the spirit burns.

And as we walk this sacred ground,
In every breath, true freedom found.
Through labyrinths of faith, ascend,
Our journey blessed, on Him depend.

The Bridge to Celestial Shores

Where faith meets the span of grace,
Hearts lifted, find their place.
On the bridge of hope we tread,
Guided by the light ahead.

Whispers of angels softly call,
As we rise, we shall not fall.
Each step leads through trials past,
In the embrace of peace, we rest.

The waters deep, yet calm they lie,
Reflecting truths that never die.
With every prayer, a path unfolds,
To celestial shores, where love beholds.

United in spirit, hand in hand,
We journey forth, a sacred band.
Through shadows dark, we find the dawn,
In unity, our fears are gone.

Oh, the bridge, a sacred grace,
To heaven's home, our destined place.
In eternal light, we find our rest,
With faith and hope, we are truly blessed.

The Beacon of Transcendence

In the night, a beacon shines bright,
Guiding souls towards the light.
With every heart, a flame ignites,
Transcending darkness, reaching heights.

Voices rise in harmony clear,
Words of truth that all can hear.
The beacon calls, unwavering,
With love and grace, it keeps on saying.

Across the seas of doubt and fear,
We gather close, for we are near.
The light unites, dispersing gloom,
In faith, we find our heart's true bloom.

A glimmer bright in endless night,
The beacon holds our dreams in sight.
With fervent hope, we seek our way,
To realms divine, a new dawn's rays.

For in each soul, a light does dwell,
In shadows thick, we weave our spell.
Bound by love, we shall transcend,
Together, forging paths, we mend.

Souls Adrift in the Cosmos

In the vast expanse, our spirits roam,
Adrift in stars, we seek a home.
Connections made across the void,
In cosmic dance, we are overjoyed.

The whispers of the universe call,
A symphony of life, embracing all.
Celestial winds, they guide our flight,
Through darkest nights, towards the light.

With every heartbeat, galaxies spin,
In the fabric of time, we are woven in.
From stardust we rise, and unto stars we yearn,
In love's embrace, our souls return.

Together we dream amidst the spheres,
Shattering doubts, dissolving fears.
In unity, we traverse the night,
With hope and love, our guiding light.

Oh, souls adrift, with purpose bright,
In the cosmos' arms, we find our sight.
Eternal seekers, hand in hand,
In this boundless realm, we shall stand.

The Keeper of Eternal Fire

In the heart of night, a flame does glow,
The keeper stands, with grace in tow.
With every spark, a story told,
Of love and warmth that break the cold.

Through trials faced, the fire remains,
A beacon bright through all the pains.
With hands outstretched, we gather near,
The keeper's gaze calms every fear.

In sacred dance, the flames do sway,
Igniting hope to light our way.
With every breath, the embers burn,
A promise made, for love's return.

For in this fire, our spirits rise,
Beneath the watchful, starry skies.
The keeper smiles, the warmth we seek,
In unity, we find our peak.

So take the light, and let it shine,
For in our hearts, the fire divine.
Together we stand, for we are strong,
In the keeper's love, we all belong.

Testament of the Stars

In the night, the heavens weep,
Whispers of secrets they keep,
Each star, a promise to behold,
Stories of ages, silently told.

Guided by light, the faithful tread,
In shadows where angels dare to spread,
The grace of the cosmos, vast and wide,
Hearts soar like comets, in truth they ride.

In prayer beneath the velvet sky,
Each fervent sigh a sacred cry,
The constellations sing their hymn,
Of hope eternal, when lights grow dim.

We gather in the celestial glow,
The pulse of eternity we know,
As mountains bow and rivers bend,
Our souls to the stars, in faith, we send.

With every dawn, the sun ignites,
A beacon of mercy, shining bright,
In the testament, we find our way,
A path of love, come what may.

A New Covenant in the Cosmos

In the silence of space, we unite,
A bond reformed in the endless night,
Galaxies spin, their dance divine,
In every star, a sign, a line.

From ashes of chaos, beauty is wrought,
In the depths of the void, hope is sought,
Each planet and moon, a sacred trust,
In the fabric of time, we must.

Vows etched in the dust of ancient skies,
The echoes of love never die,
In each heartbeat, a cosmic grace,
A new covenant, finding its place.

As meteors fall, we raise our hands,
Offering dreams to divine lands,
With each breath taken, a prayer is cast,
In the light of the future, we're free at last.

In unity, let our spirits soar,
Together we rise, forevermore,
A journey of faith, beyond all strife,
In the heart of the cosmos, we find our life.

Beneath the Weeping Willow

In shadows soft, the willow weeps,
Guarding the dreams that the heart keeps,
Beneath its branches, the weary rest,
In nature's arms, they are blessed.

The rustling leaves, a soothing breath,
Whispers of life, defying death,
Each droplet falling, a story to share,
Of love and loss, of how we care.

In the quiet dusk, we find our peace,
By the water's edge, our fears decrease,
Through tangled roots, our paths entwine,
In the sacred silence, we align.

Under the stars, we offer our dreams,
To the night sky, where starlight gleams,
A promise made beneath the tree,
In every tear, a sacred plea.

As dawn awakes, the shadows fade,
The weeping willow, a love displayed,
In every breeze, we feel anew,
A bond unbroken, forever true.

Threads of Divinity in the Abyss

In the depths where shadows lie,
Threads of light weave through the sky,
In the abyss, a sacred thread,
Binding the lost, the broken led.

Whispers of mercy brush the soul,
Healing the wounds, making us whole,
In every heart, a spark ignites,
Banishing darkness, bringing light.

Through trials faced and storms endured,
In the silence, our faith assured,
Each challenge met, a gift we bear,
The threads of divinity, our prayer.

In the tapestry of the divine,
Each life a note, in harmony's line,
Together we rise, breaking the chain,
In the depths of despair, we find our gain.

In every heartbeat, a promise lies,
A testament to the skies,
From the abyss, we emerge, we sing,
Threads of divinity, our offering.

The Oracle of Reflections

In quiet pools, truths arise,
Mirrors of the soul, so wise.
Glimmers of fate within the deep,
Awakening secrets, in silence, we keep.

The whispers call, urging to see,
Paths untraveled, set our hearts free.
Each vision clear, a sacred sign,
Guiding us towards the divine.

Hands raised in reverence, we stand,
In the light of wisdom, we understand.
An oracle's voice, tender and bold,
Revealing the stories yet to be told.

With every ripple, the truth unfolds,
In moments of stillness, the spirit beholds.
Echoes of grace, in the depths flow,
The oracle speaks, in the heart's glow.

In this sacred realm, we are one,
Reflecting the wonders of the sun.
In solitude's gaze, we find our way,
Embracing the night, welcoming Day.

The Light That Never Fades

In shadows cast, a glow remains,
A beacon bright through all of our pains.
With every heart, its warmth ignites,
Binding the souls, in sacred rites.

A gentle whisper, a call from above,
Unveiling the depths of infinite love.
Through trials faced, the light will guide,
Eternal presence, forever beside.

As dawn breaks forth, shadows retreat,
The light awakens, our spirits complete.
In every promise, its truth we find,
A hope everlasting, transcending time.

Through valleys low and mountains grand,
The light leads onward, hand in hand.
With every breath, we rise anew,
In the grace of love, our spirits flew.

In every heart, the light will soar,
A promise of peace, forevermore.
Through every trial, it will invade,
With faith as our armor, we're never afraid.

Whispers of the Divine

In the stillness of the night,
Soft voices murmur with pure light.
Guiding us through the shadows' sway,
Whispers of love show us the way.

With gentle breath, the spirits call,
In every heartbeat, we feel it all.
A sacred dance, the soul aligns,
In every moment, the divine shines.

Through tangled paths and winding roads,
Each whisper carries, lifting our loads.
As nature hums, the world awakens,
In the sacred hush, our fears are shaken.

Transcending realms, the veil grows thin,
In the heart's quiet, we find our kin.
Voices of angels, soft and clear,
In every breath, the divine is near.

With every step, we seek and learn,
In each whisper, the world will turn.
Trust in the path that unfolds below,
In whispers of the divine, we grow.

Beyond the Threshold of Existence

At the edge of dreams, we find our fate,
Crossing the threshold, it's never too late.
In realms unknown, our spirit flies,
Beyond the veil where eternity lies.

With open hearts, we dare to tread,
Into the unknown, where angels have led.
In sacred whispers, the truth unveiled,
Through love's great journey, we are regaled.

On this bridge, where life intertwines,
Awakening souls, through love's designs.
Each step we take, a promise bestowed,
Beyond the limits, our spirits explode.

In cosmic dance, we embrace the light,
Navigating darkness with pure delight.
Here in the stillness, we find our way,
Beyond the threshold, into the day.

In the embrace of the infinite span,
We discover the fullness of who we am.
Beyond all worries, we stand as one,
In the heart of existence, our journey begun.

Threads of Faith in a Fractured World

In shadows deep, our spirits rise,
With whispered prayers that pierce the skies.
Each heart a thread, woven tight,
Faith remains our guiding light.

Through storms of doubt, we stand as one,
With hope ablaze, our battles won.
In every tear and joyful song,
The thread of faith makes us strong.

In fractured times, we seek the whole,
Embracing love to heal the soul.
With every deed, and every breath,
We weave a tapestry from death.

The hands unite, a sacred bond,
A voice of peace, our hearts respond.
Each gentle act, a treasured gift,
In faith's embrace, we find our lift.

So let us walk on paths divine,
With threads of faith, our souls entwine.
In every trial, we shall not yield,
For love and hope become our shield.

Voices of the Ancients

In whispered tales, the ancients speak,
Of love and loss, the strong and weak.
Their wisdom flows like rivers wide,
In hearts of seekers, they abide.

Echoes of laughter, shadows of sorrow,
The past unfolds, a bright tomorrow.
With every step, we walk their paths,
In sacred circles, their wisdom lasts.

From sacred texts to starlit skies,
They teach us truths that never die.
Through trials faced and battles fought,
In every lesson, gratitude taught.

The spirits guide through darkened nights,
With gentle hands, they spark the lights.
Each voice a melody, pure and sweet,
In unity, our hearts repeat.

Though time may fade, their echoes stay,
As we walk forth, come what may.
In every prayer, in every song,
The voices of the ancients throng.

Tapestry of the Unseen

In every thread, a story weaves,
A tapestry that never leaves.
Beyond the veil, where spirits play,
The unseen world, our hearts' ballet.

In silent whispers, we find the ties,
Where love transcends, and never dies.
The colors swirl in sacred dance,
Each moment holds a timeless chance.

Through woven dreams, our visions gleam,
In fleeting moments, life may seem.
Yet under currents, deep and wide,
We journey forth, with faith as guide.

With every heartbeat, every prayer,
We touch the fabric, beyond compare.
The unseen threads unite us all,
In love's embrace, we rise, we fall.

Through trials faced and paths unknown,
In sacred spaces, we have grown.
In every heartbeat, every sigh,
The tapestry whispers, never die.

Covenant of the Silent

In quiet moments, we gather near,
A covenant born from hope and fear.
With silent vows, we pledge our souls,
In faith we stand, as heartbeats roll.

Through stillness deep, the spirit calls,
In hushed tones shared, the silence falls.
Each breath a promise, unspoken truth,
In sacred bonds, we reclaim our youth.

Beneath the stars, we softly pray,
For healing grace to light the way.
In gentle hearts, our faith ignites,
A covenant forged in tranquil nights.

Though words may fade, the feelings grow,
In every spirit, love will flow.
With trust entwined, we journey forth,
In silent strength, we find our worth.

Together we stand, in peace we bind,
A covenant of hearts entwined.
Through every trial and peaceful night,
In silent faith, we reach the light.

The Light that Illuminates the Void

In shadows deep where silence dwells,
A beacon shines, sweet grace compels.
With whispers soft, the spirit calls,
To lift the heart when darkness falls.

From depths of night, the dawn breaks clear,
Its radiant glow, a gift sincere.
Each flicker bright, a promise made,
In love's embrace, all fears will fade.

Though trials come, and storms may rage,
Divine embrace turns every page.
In every tear, a lesson learned,
As sacred fires within us burned.

A path unfolds, through pain we find,
Eternal truths that bind mankind.
In unity, we rise and cling,
To harmony that life can bring.

Oh, light that shines in endless night,
Guide weary souls toward the right.
For in your glow, we come alive,
Together here, we shall survive.

Dance of the Celestial Spirits

In heavens high, the stars convene,
Celestial waltz, both bright and keen.
With silver rays, they weave and sway,
In cosmic rhythm, night turns to day.

Each twinkle holds a tale untold,
Of ancient wisdom, brave and bold.
The spirits dance on winds of grace,
In harmony, we find our place.

With every note, their voices rise,
In sacred song that never dies.
They guide our hearts through dark and light,
Their loving gaze, a steady sight.

From dawn to dusk, they twirl and glide,
In unity, they take their ride.
Their laughter echoes through the skies,
A symphony that never lies.

In every heart, their essence dwells,
A sacred bond that time compels.
So let us join this joyful spree,
Souls intertwined, forever free.

Elysium Awaits

In gardens rich, where blossoms bloom,
The fragrance soft dispels all gloom.
With petals bright, and skies so wide,
In Elysium, our hearts abide.

A tranquil stream flows crystal clear,
It sings of peace, dispelling fear.
The golden sun caresses all,
In life's embrace, we rise, we fall.

Each path we tread leads closer still,
To realms of joy where hearts can fill.
In every heartbeat, love's refrain,
A balm for every ounce of pain.

The light of faith, a guiding star,
Illuminates just who we are.
In unity, our spirits soar,
Together here, forevermore.

So take my hand, we'll journey hence,
To fields of gold, where love makes sense.
In Elysium, we shall unite,
In sacred dreams, our souls take flight.

Beyond the Silent Veil

In whispers soft where shadows blend,
The sacred veil begins to bend.
Through stillness deep, a voice is clear,
Inviting all to draw quite near.

Beyond the silence, grace awaits,
In every heartbeat, love creates.
The secrets held in time's embrace,
Reveal the truth of sacred space.

As spirits roam in twilight's glow,
They guide us gently, soft and slow.
In every tear, shared hope resides,
Through every loss, the heart abides.

So lift your eyes and seek the light,
Beyond the veil, find pure delight.
In union, we will find our way,
As night gives birth to a new day.

Oh, see the dawn where shadows fade,
In love's embrace, our souls cascade.
Together here, we cast aside,
The silent veil, with arms spread wide.

The Promise of Endless Morning

In dawn's embrace, hope's light ignites,
The shadows flee, as day takes flight.
With every beam, grace overflows,
A promise kept, as the spirit grows.

The heart anew, in faith awakes,
Through valleys deep, the journey takes.
In whispered prayers, we find our strength,
A love that spans the endless length.

From darkest night, we rise and soar,
With courage bold, our souls restore.
The sun ascends, in glory shines,
A beacon bright, through endless times.

In every moment, blessings fall,
Each breath a gift, our spirits call.
With arms outstretched, we greet the morn,
In every heart, forever sworn.

So let us walk in faith divine,
Embracing light, as hearts entwine.
In unity, our voices sing,
The promise forged, in the joy we bring.

Celestial Hymn of the Redeemed

From depths of sorrow, we arise,
With hearts uplifted to the skies.
Each note resounds, in sacred space,
A hymn of love, our souls embrace.

The stars above, in chorus ring,
As angels dance and praises sing.
In melody, our spirits soar,
United strong, forevermore.

Through trials faced, we find our way,
In light of hope, we cease to sway.
The gift of grace, so freely given,
A path to peace, our hearts are driven.

With every tear, a lesson learned,
Through darkest nights, our faith discerned.
In unity, we gather near,
Our voices raised, in love sincere.

For every soul, a story told,
In the warmth of love, we break the mold.
So let the hymn resound and fill,
In every heart, the sacred will.

Silent Reflections in Sacred Space

In quiet corners, wisdom grows,
Where stillness reigns, the spirit flows.
Each whispered thought, a prayer in flight,
A journey deep, through veils of light.

The sacred space, a tranquil ground,
Where grace abounds and love is found.
In every sigh, a truth unveils,
In silence, peace, our heart prevails.

Amidst the trials, hope remains,
In silent moments, joy sustains.
Through every tear, we learn to see,
The beauty wrapped in mystery.

A sacred bond, with every breath,
In stillness felt, transcending death.
In quietude, our spirits mend,
In silent prayer, we find a friend.

So let us dwell in places pure,
With hearts open wide, our faith ensures.
In sacred silence, peace shall bloom,
With love surrounding, dispelling gloom.

The Altar of the Dispossessed

In shadows cast by sorrow's hand,
The dispossessed, a faithful band.
In every loss, a longing prayer,
A heart that yearns, a spirit rare.

With open arms, we gather near,
In shared despair, we shed a tear.
Each story told, a testament,
To strength found deep, in grace's scent.

The altar built on love and pain,
Through struggles faced, our souls remain.
In unity, we rise anew,
With hearts ablaze, our spirits true.

In every tear, a sacred vow,
To stand as one, in this we bow.
For every wound, a healing touch,
In love's embrace, we find as much.

So let us honor those in need,
With open hearts, we plant the seed.
In kindness shared, a light shall shine,
The altar forged, in love's design.

The Radiance of Forgotten Paths

In shadows deep where silence reigns,
The spirit calls, it softly claims.
A light that flickers through the veil,
Whispers of hope upon the trail.

The weary traveler finds their way,
With faith as guide both night and day.
Every step on sacred ground,
A resurrection's voice is found.

The heart beats true, a sacred drum,
In wild, lost places, life will come.
Awake the dreams within the dust,
In every path, there's sacred trust.

The echoes call, with gentle grace,
As dawn unveils the hidden space.
A map of stars, in night's embrace,
Each twist and turn, His love we chase.

Remember well these paths once lost,
For every journey bears its cost.
In twilight's glow, we rise anew,
In humble hearts, His light shines through.

A Tapestry of Resilience

We weave our sorrows, thread of gold,
Stitched with the tales of those of old.
In every struggle, stories bloom,
From darkest nights, hope finds its room.

The loom of life, frail hands entwine,
Each knot a lesson, every line.
Through storms that rage, and trials that break,
The art of healing, we awake.

With every fray, a patch is sewn,
In love and faith, we are not alone.
A vibrant hue from gray and black,
Each tear a badge, no looking back.

The fabric speaks of love and loss,
Of burdens borne and the faithful cross.
With courage stitched in every seam,
We rise, reborn, into the dream.

Together we stand, a mural bright,
In unity, we face the night.
With light that binds, we'll always mend,
This tapestry of life, we'll defend.

Seraphic Echoes in the Stillness

In quietude the angels sing,
Their voices blend in whispered wing.
A serenade for souls that seek,
The light of truth, the hope we speak.

Among the stars, their glow does weave,
A tapestry of love we believe.
Each note a balm for weary hearts,
A healing grace that never departs.

In moments hushed, the spirit flows,
The sacred dance, where kindness grows.
Through silent prayers, divine sparks fly,
In stillness hear the angels' cry.

They trace the paths of those who roam,
Guiding the lost, leading them home.
With gentle hands, they mold the clay,
In every breath, they pave the way.

As twilight falls and darkness swells,
The seraphs cast their subtle spells.
In peace, we find our hearts align,
Listen closely; the soul shall shine.

Celestial Revelations at Twilight

When day meets night, the heavens sigh,
The painted sky, our spirits fly.
In twilight's glow, the stars unfold,
Stories of love, in whispers told.

The sun dips low, a golden dream,
While shadows stretch, a mystic theme.
Each star a thought, each breeze a prayer,
In silence born, divinity's care.

With every dusk, the veil grows thin,
Revealing wonders deep within.
In sacred spaces, hearts ignite,
Mysteries dance in the fading light.

Across the skies, the angels roam,
Their laughter carries us back home.
Each twinkle holds a vast embrace,
In every breath, we seek His grace.

As night descends, our spirits rise,
In celestial tales, the wisdom lies.
Awake the dawn, in faith we trust,
For every ending births a new gust.

Chronicles of the Undying Flame

In the heart of shadows, a light still stays,
Guiding the lost through the darkest maze.
With whispers of hope and embers of grace,
The undying flame lifts the weary face.

Through trials and storms, its warmth remains,
Binding the spirit as love sustains.
Each flicker a promise, each spark a song,
The flame will endure, steadfast and strong.

When the night is heavy and courage fades,
It speaks soft truths in luminous shades.
In every heart, a spark ignites,
Together we rise, chasing the lights.

Let the wind carry tales on its breath,
Of souls united beyond the death.
With faith as our anchor, we'll stand as one,
For the undying flame will never be done.

Litanies of Lost Souls

In the silence of night, the whispers arise,
Litanies echo beneath starlit skies.
Souls once shining, now muted in flight,
In grief and in longing, they seek the light.

Each cry a reminder of dreams left behind,
The fragile hopes that the dark intertwined.
Yet from the shadows, the hymns softly call,
A gentle refrain for the lost, for us all.

Beneath the moon's watch, they weave and they sway,
Guiding the weary along the lost way.
In their lament, a beauty unfolds,
The litanies echo, a tale to be told.

Hold close their memories, the love that remains,
For lost souls are tethered in joy and in pains.
In dreams they'll return, together we'll stand,
In this sacred dance, heart to heart, hand in hand.

Transcendence Through Time's Grasp

Beneath the vast canopy of ancient skies,
Time weaves its tales where the spirit flies.
In moments of stillness, we touch the divine,
Transcendence unfolds in the heart's quiet line.

Each tick of the clock holds a sacred embrace,
Whispers of wisdom in life's lively trace.
Beyond the horizon where seconds retreat,
In silence, the echoes of love form a fleet.

Seasons turn gently, like pages of fate,
With each fleeting breath, we learn to await.
In the depths of our souls, the answers reside,
Transcendence, a journey, where peace will abide.

Through life's fragile tapestry, woven with care,
We find strength in the moments we've chosen to share.
In the grasp of the time, we are evermore,
Embraced by the essence of what we adore.

Anointed by the Falling Stars

From the heavens above, the stars gently fall,
Carrying blessings, they whisper to all.
Anointed in light, our spirits embrace,
The magic of night brings peace to our space.

Each shimmering spark is a dream to behold,
A promise of hope in the stories we've told.
In their dance through the sky, they weep and they gleam,

Guiding us softly, like a lullaby dream.

With wishes on lips, we call to the night,
Embracing the journey, guided by light.
In unity's grace, we'll gather the flames,
Anointed by stardust, we'll never be the same.

The cosmos sings loudly, in vibrant refrains,
Telling of love that forever remains.
As falling stars twinkle, we cherish the thrill,
Anointed by dreams, our hearts ever still.

The New Covenant: Hope's Embers

In the silence of night, we gather round,
A promise renewed, in His love we're bound.
With hearts aflame, we whisper and pray,
For the dawn of His grace to light our way.

In shadows of doubt, His glory shines bright,
Guiding our steps through the dark into light.
A covenant forged in the blood of the Lamb,
Hope's embers ignited, forever we stand.

Each tear that we shed, a seed of His care,
In each whispered plea, we find solace there.
The old has now passed, behold, we are new,
In the midst of our struggles, His love will break through.

With faith as our anchor, we dare to believe,
For every lost soul, His heart will retrieve.
Expectations soaring, our spirits will rise,
In the New Covenant's grace, no need for disguise.

So we walk on this path, hand in hand with the meek,
With hope as our banner, it's love that we seek.
The embers of promise, they flicker and glow,
In the folds of His mercy, our spirits will grow.

Blessings in the Shadow of Despair

In the depths of night, when hope seems to fade,
We cling to the light that will never evade.
Every tear that we shed, a story untold,
In the shadow of sorrow, our faith will hold gold.

The trials we face, like shadows, they loom,
Yet blessings unfold in the midst of our gloom.
A whisper of grace in the silence we find,
In the heart of the struggle, our spirits unwind.

With gratitude's eye, we see through the pain,
The beauty in chaos, the sun after rain.
For every dark moment, there's light on the way,
In the shadow of despair, hope carves out a ray.

So let us embrace every tear that does fall,
Each moment a gift, we surrender it all.
In the garden of trials, let joy take its flight,
For blessings may blossom, even in night.

Together we'll rise from the ashes of dread,
With faith as our compass, where angels have tread.
In the shadow of despair, our hearts will proclaim,
That love is the victor, forever the same.

Traces of Divinity

Each raindrop that falls carries whispers of grace,
In the dance of the leaves, we behold His face.
The stars in the night, like diamonds, align,
In traces of divinity, His love we define.

The mountains that rise, steadfast and bold,
Tell tales of His strength in the beauty they hold.
Across endless skies, His promise does weave,
In every deep valley, we learn to believe.

The laughter of children, the warmth of the sun,
In the moments of bliss, His presence is spun.
In kindness bestowed, and in hearts that are true,
We find the reflections of Him in the new.

In silence, we hear the soft call of the heart,
The traces of love that will never depart.
For every small gesture, for every kind deed,
In lives intertwined, divinity's seed.

So open your eyes to the beauty around,
In the ordinary moments, His grace will abound.
In traces of divinity, we find our way home,
In the fabric of life, we are never alone.

A Spirit's Journey Through Darkness

Through valleys of shadows, a spirit does tread,
In the depths of the night where even hope fled.
With courage as armor, and faith as a shield,
In the battle of night, it's the heart that won't yield.

Each step is a prayer, a whisper of love,
Guided by stars that shine brightly above.
The path may grow weary, the weight we can bear,
For the light of tomorrow brings solace and care.

In the echoes of silence, the spirit takes flight,
Transforming the darkness into heavenly light.
The struggles we face are but shadows in time,
For within every trial, the spirit will climb.

With every dark moment, a lesson unfolds,
A journey of healing, a story retold.
Embrace every tear, let them wash you anew,
In the spirit's great journey, we find what is true.

So here in the darkness, let us find grace,
For the dawn is approaching, and we shall embrace.
In the spirit's own journey, together we find,
That the light shines the brightest, where love is defined.

The Book of Unwritten Futures

In shadows deep where whispers dwell,
The ink of fate begins to swell,
Each page a choice, each breath a chance,
A dance of dreams in silent trance.

The scribes above with watchful eyes,
In moments bare, in secret skies,
They carve the paths of hearts anew,
For every soul, a journey true.

With every tear, a lesson learned,
With every joy, a fire burned,
The chapters weave through time and space,
Each heartbeat sings of grace embraced.

In the quiet dusk, a spark ignites,
The future waits in sacred lights,
Awake, arise to dreams untold,
In faith, we grasp the hands of gold.

So write the words, let spirits soar,
In the book of life, forevermore,
With love as ink, let hope prevail,
For every future tells a tale.

The Ascending Spirit

In the stillness of the night,
A spirit calls in softest light,
It lifts us up, it guides our way,
Through shadows deep to break of day.

With wings of faith and hearts of fire,
We reach for truth, inspired, higher,
The echoes hum of past divine,
In unity, our souls align.

Let doubts disperse like mist at dawn,
With every step, a life reborn,
The climbing voice of love's decree,
In harmony, we cease to flee.

We rise above the stormy seas,
Embraced by grace, we find our peace,
Ascend we shall, beyond the stars,
In endless light, through open bars.

For every heart that seeks the sky,
In every whisper, hear the sigh,
The spirit dances, wild and free,
In realms of joy, eternally.

When the Earth Breathed Again

In twilight hours, a sigh was shared,
The earth awoke, her heart laid bare,
With whispered trees and flowing streams,
She spoke of life in waking dreams.

The mountains echoed ancient words,
In rustling leaves, the song of birds,
The rivers flowed with stories grand,
As nature's voice kissed every land.

With every bloom, a promise bright,
In colors soft, the day takes flight,
From ashes rise the seeds of hope,
In gentle wraps, we learn to cope.

When seasons change and shadows fall,
The earth, she sings, unites us all,
Her breath a balm for weary souls,
In her embrace, the spirit strolls.

So hear the call, let love remain,
For when the earth breathed once again,
A cycle spun in endless grace,
In her sweet heart, we find our place.

Light Through the Cracks of Time

In days gone by, when shadows loom,
A flicker breaks the tightening gloom,
Through cracks of time, a vision glows,
A hope ignites, the spirit knows.

With every dawn, a chance to see,
The light that sets our spirits free,
In fractured moments, wisdom shines,
The hands of fate draw sacred lines.

Let courage rise with every breath,
In trials faced, defying death,
For through the pain, we seek the light,
In tender hearts, love's pure insight.

Eternal truth, we yearn to find,
In broken dreams, we're intertwined,
For every shadow has a source,
In light and dark, we find our course.

Embrace the cracks that time bestows,
In each soft glow, our spirit grows,
For in the dark, we'll learn to see,
That light is love, in unity.

The Flame of the Unconquered

In the heart a flame ignites,
Unyielding strength through darkest nights.
With every breath, a whispered prayer,
A beacon bright, our souls laid bare.

The trials faced, a sacred rite,
In unity, we find our light.
The spirits guide our steadfast way,
In faith we stand, come what may.

Through tempests wild and shadows deep,
The flame within, our promise we keep.
With courage found in love's embrace,
We rise above, we find our place.

Each heartbeat sings a sacred song,
Together we are brave and strong.
The flame of hope, it burns so bright,
In darkness' grasp, we are the light.

With open arms to future's call,
We stand as one, we will not fall.
The flame of the unconquered glows,
In peace and power, love still grows.

The Light That Beckons

A distant star, it calls to me,
A whisper on the evening sea.
In shadows cast by doubt and fear,
The light that beckons draws me near.

Through winding paths and trials vast,
I seek the truth, the die is cast.
In every moment, grace bestowed,
The light that shines, the way I'm showed.

With open heart, I journey on,
In every dusk awaits the dawn.
The light of hope, it lifts the veil,
In sacred trust, I will prevail.

As silence falls and stars arise,
I breathe the peace that never dies.
The light that beckons, pure and clear,
In love eternal, I draw near.

With faith renewed, I walk this road,
In every burden, there's a load.
The light that calls, forever bright,
In darkest hour, it leads to light.

Guardians of the Ethereal Dawn

In twilight's grace, we stand as one,
Guardians true 'til day is done.
With hearts entwined, our spirits soar,
Together we guard this sacred shore.

Each heartbeat echoes through the night,
Bound by love, held fast in light.
With eyes that see beyond the veil,
Guardians brave, we shall not fail.

In whispers soft, the dawn appears,
We cast aside our doubts and fears.
With strength renewed, we rise to greet,
The ethereal dawn, pure and sweet.

With fervent hearts, we share this space,
In every breath, we find His grace.
Guardians of hope, we walk the line,
In sacred trust, our souls align.

Through trials faced, we stand so tall,
In unity, we answer the call.
Guardians of the dawn's embrace,
Together we'll forever trace.

Odes to the Once Forgotten

In memories lost, we find our way,
Odes to those who went astray.
Their voices rise, a tender song,
In hearts we hold, they still belong.

Through whispered prayers, we honor deep,
The tales they told, the dreams they keep.
In gentle light, their spirits shine,
Odes to the ones who crossed the line.

From dusk 'til dawn, their stories weave,
In every breath, we love, believe.
With every tear that paints the night,
Odes to their journey take their flight.

In shadows cast, their memories wade,
An eternal bond shall never fade.
For in the heart, their music plays,
Odes to the once forgotten days.

As seasons change and time moves on,
We carry forth their light, life's song.
Embraced by love, we will not part,
Odes to the souls forever in heart.

In the Wake of Shadows

In the twilight's gentle hush,
Whispers rise like softened sighs,
Guided by a holy rush,
Hope ignites as darkness flies.

In each heart, a spark resides,
Faith like stars in velvet skies,
Though the night may be our guide,
Light will break, our spirit flies.

Casting fears into the deep,
We stand firm 'neath heaven's gaze,
Every promise, we shall keep,
In the dawn, our hearts will blaze.

Shadows bow to morning's grace,
As we rise, our souls awake,
Together in this holy place,
In love's name, our chains will break.

Stripped of doubt, we find our way,
In the wake of shadows cast,
With each prayer, we learn to sway,
Towards the light that's meant to last.

The Light Beyond the Ruins

Upon the ashes, hope will bloom,
From shattered stone, the spirit soars,
In every heart that faced the gloom,
A voice whispers of open doors.

Through tangled paths of desolation,
We hold on to our sacred grace,
In the depths of tribulation,
The light calls forth, a warm embrace.

Every ruin tells a story,
Of battles fought and lessons learned,
In darkest nights, behold the glory,
For in loss, new paths are turned.

Together we stand, hand in hand,
With faith our guide, we journey far,
From broken ground, we gently stand,
Illuminated by love's star.

As dawn breaks on a starlit dream,
We rise anew from yesterday,
Into the light, a boundless beam,
Beyond the ruins, we find our way.

Resurrection of Forgotten Dreams

In silence deep, the dreams await,
Nurtured by the streams of time,
With open arms, they celebrate,
The chance to rise, our hearts in rhyme.

From shadows cast by doubt and fear,
We call forth visions once held dear,
In every tear, there's strength to find,
Reviving hopes that fate entwined.

With whispered prayers that cross the night,
We summon dreams to take their flight,
For every soul deserves to soar,
And tread the paths of love once more.

In unity, our voices blend,
A symphony of lives restored,
Together we shall transcend,
Each heartbeat echoing the Lord.

A resurrection strong and bright,
From ashes forged, our spirits gleam,
No longer bound by fear's dark night,
We rise anew — alive, we dream.

The Last Prayer of the Wanderer

On weary roads, my feet have traced,
Through deserts dry and mountains steep,
A wanderer seeking love's embrace,
In every shadow, secrets keep.

Beneath the stars, my heart did call,
With every step, I sought the light,
In whispered prayers, I found my all,
Through darkest paths, I won the fight.

The echoes of my distant cries,
Resound like thunder in the night,
Yet in my soul, sweet comfort lies,
For grace will guide me towards the right.

In gratitude, I bow my head,
The last prayer lingers like a song,
For every hurt, and every dread,
Will lead me where I now belong.

So here I stand, my heart laid bare,
The final wish, a silent plea,
That all my journeys, all my care,
Will find me home, eternally.

Forgiveness in the Wake of Silence

In stillness lies the heart's release,
A whispered prayer, a quiet peace.
In shadows cast by tarnished days,
We find the light in gentle ways.

Forgiving hands extend so wide,
With grace that swells like rising tide.
Each burden lifted in His name,
Awakens hope, extinguishes shame.

The soul's sweet song, both soft and strong,
Leads back to love where we belong.
In silence, bonds of trust renew,
In every heart, forgiveness, too.

Let echoes of our past disperse,
As mercy flows, we break the curse.
In unity, we find our way,
A sacred path to brighter day.

So let our hearts be vessels pure,
For love distilled, and faith secure.
In every sigh, in every plea,
Forgiveness blooms eternally.

The Covenant of the Reborn

In waters deep, we lay our past,
Emerging bright, our hearts amassed.
In sacred bonds, we rise anew,
The covenant's light, forever true.

From ashes gray to vibrant dawn,
In faith renewed, we carry on.
With gentle hands, we shape the clay,
A vessel strong for love's display.

Every heartbeat sings of grace,
In every trial, we find our place.
The reborn soul, a beacon's glow,
Illuminating paths we sow.

We walk united, hand in hand,
Together in this promised land.
Each step we take, a sacred vow,
The journey blessed, this moment now.

Through storms we face, and tempests rise,
Our spirits soar beyond the skies.
In every trial, our faith adorned,
We celebrate the covenant, reborn.

Sacred Footprints on Dusty Paths

Upon the earth, our traces dwell,
In every step, a tale to tell.
With humble hearts, we walk the way,
In sacred footprints, we will stay.

Through winding roads and valleys low,
We follow where the Spirit flows.
Each grain of dust, a lesson learned,
In gentle light, our souls discerned.

In moments dark, a compass bright,
Guides us toward the purest light.
With every breath, we seek to find,
The truth that speaks to heart and mind.

To share our burdens, hand in hand,
We weave a tapestry so grand.
In every laugh, in every tear,
The sacred path grows strong and clear.

For on this journey, we must tread,
With loving grace and hope ahead.
Each footprint marks a love profound,
In dusty paths, our faith is found.

Embracing the Eternal Emptiness

In silence, we embrace the void,
A sacred space, untouched, untied.
Here in the stillness, we shall find,
The breadth of love that knows no kind.

As shadows wane and light takes hold,
The emptiness becomes our gold.
With open hearts, we breathe the air,
In every longing, in every prayer.

It is not loss, but room to grow,
In barren lands, new seeds we sow.
For in the quiet, voices swell,
In every story, a truth to tell.

Thus we embrace what seems unfilled,
With faith and courage, hearts are thrilled.
The eternal dance of give and take,
In empty spaces, we awake.

In every heartbeat, every sigh,
We learn to love, we learn to fly.
With open hands and spirits bright,
We find our peace in boundless light.

Heavens Unfolding

In stillness, whispers rise,
A choir of celestial light.
Stars awaken, skies ignite,
Faith ascends to boundless heights.

Wings of angels softly bend,
Guiding souls through night's embrace.
Each prayer a spark, a transcend,
We find our home in sacred space.

Search the depths, and gaze above,
In shadows, hope begins to bloom.
Divine grace, like gentle love,
Dissolves despair, dispels the gloom.

Voices echo through the spheres,
A melody of peace bestowed.
With every heartbeat, cast out fears,
Hearts aflame with love's abode.

In unison, we rise as one,
Hearts entwined in the divine.
Our journey shines beneath the sun,
In heaven's arms, we intertwine.

When Time Meets Infinity

In silence where the moments blend,
Eternity whispers without end.
The clock unwinds in timeless grace,
As dawn unfolds a sacred space.

Every heartbeat, a drop in streams,
Flowing towards the realm of dreams.
Infinite paths before our eyes,
Guiding us through sacred skies.

Echoes linger in the air,
Hope awakened with each prayer.
The past and future intertwine,
In this embrace, we find the divine.

Time, a river, vast and free,
Washes over, sets us free.
Lost in wonder, we break the mold,
In love's embrace, we're gently told.

Together, we reach for the light,
As souls unite in endless flight.
With every breath, we bridge the span,
When time meets infinity, we began.

The Covenant of New Beginnings

In the dawn of creation's breath,
A promise carved beyond our death.
Every sunrise, hope reborn,
In union, hearts are gently worn.

Seeds of faith are sown anew,
With every step, we seek the true.
A covenant wrapped in sacred grace,
Embracing change, each face we trace.

Through trials faced, we find our song,
Together where the brave belong.
With each sunset, the shadows fall,
A testament to love's great call.

Hand in hand, we journey ahead,
Where angels fear to tread.
In humble hearts, the light will shine,
In every ending, a grand design.

With open spirits, we rise anew,
A covenant, vibrant and true.
Eternally bound in love's embrace,
In this dance, we find our place.

In the Embrace of the Unseen

Within the veil, the spirit speaks,
In whispers soft, the heart seeks.
Hidden paths in shadows coil,
In faith, we find our sacred soil.

The breath of silence fills the night,
With unseen hands guiding our flight.
Divine presence, ever near,
Each moment wrapped in love sincere.

In stillness, we behold the grace,
Reflections dance, their soft embrace.
A gentle pull, beyond our view,
In every heartbeat, the sacred true.

As stars align in cosmic sway,
The heart remembers, finds its way.
In the unseen, the light reveals,
A bond of love, that deeply heals.

Together, we walk this hallowed ground,
In every silence, our faith is found.
In the unseen, we find our song,
A symphony where we all belong.

Milton Keynes UK
Ingram Content Group UK Ltd.
UKHW020041271124
451585UK00012B/982